Keeping Well

Written by Frances James
Series Consultant: Linda Hoyt

WorldWise™
Content-based Learning

Contents

Chapter 1

A happy, healthy life

There are many things we need to keep well. We need clean, safe drinking water and healthy food. We need to live in a clean environment. We also have to exercise regularly to keep fit, and have **vaccinations** so we won't get harmful diseases. If we feel safe and have people around who love us, we will be happier and healthier.

Some things we need to stay healthy

Water

clean, safe water free from harmful substances

Food

healthy food and regular meals; food stored away from flies and other insects; refrigeration to keep food fresh and safe

Shelter

clean, dry and warm home with bathroom

Rachel is nine years old. She lives a happy, healthy life because her parents make sure that:

- she lives in a safe home

- she gets enough fresh food to eat and clean water to drink

- she has vaccinations to prevent disease.

Feelings

having love and friendship; feeling safe and accepted

Prevention

staying fit, getting enough sleep, being vaccinated and taking medicine when needed

Did you know?

We spend about one-third of our lives asleep, and sleeping is very important when it comes to our health. Sleep refreshes us, increases our efficiency, helps us to overcome illness and can even increase our life span.

Looking back

When Rachel's grandmother and great-grandmother were children, the chances of getting seriously ill were higher than they are now. This was because many of the things that help keep Rachel healthy had not yet been invented or discovered, or were not widely available.

 Did you know?

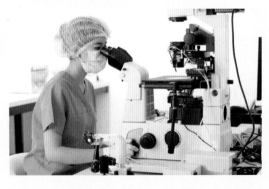

In 1932 the invention of the electron microscope helped scientists to see inside cells from the human body and identify the **bacteria** that cause many diseases.

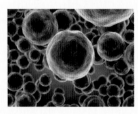

One bacteria cell can multiply to become one million cells in just 12 hours.

Charlotte
(Rachel's great-grandmother)

Born: 1921 in Manchester, England

Living conditions: Charlotte was born into a large family who lived together in a two-bedroom house. The house had cold running water, but there were no indoor bathrooms. Refrigerators were not available.

Health: About the time Charlotte was born, a dangerous type of influenza swept across the world, killing more than 25 million people. Charlotte's older sister died of tuberculosis when she was 16, and her brother died of whooping cough when he was a baby. Charlotte got plenty of exercise. People walked more than they do now, and they also worked hard doing chores.

Estimated length of life: 63 years

Emily
(Rachel's grandmother)

Born: 1941 in Sydney, Australia

Living conditions: Emily's family had six people who lived together in a three-bedroom house. The house had cold running water and an indoor bathroom with a water heater. Emily's family had a refrigerator.

Health: When Emily was born, her five-year-old sister caught pneumonia. She was given the newly discovered **antibiotic** drug penicillin, which helped her get better. When Emily was three, there was an outbreak of polio. Many children got sick and some died. Although Emily's family had a car, she and her brothers and sisters got lots of exercise because they still walked to school, to visit friends and to the shops.

Estimated length of life: 70 years

Rachel

Born: Nine years ago in Perth, Australia

Living conditions: Rachel lives with her mum, dad and brother in a three-bedroom house. The house has hot and cold running water. Her family has a refrigerator and a freezer.

Health: Rachel has had vaccinations against the diseases that were a threat to her great-grandmother's health, and many medicines are available if she gets ill. The main threat to Rachel's health is a lack of exercise. Many children are overweight because they don't get enough exercise and they eat too many sugary, fatty foods.
There has also been an increase in allergies caused by reactions to dust, pollen, some foods, animal stings and pollution.

Estimated length of life: 86 years

Chapter 2

Preventing illness

Did you know?

When harmful organisms enter your body, your immune system makes antibodies. These antibodies remove the organisms from your body.

When we are happy and healthy, our bodies are amazingly strong and capable. Even so, there are harmful **viruses**, **bacteria** and other organisms in the environment that can cause infections and disease. The human body has its own built-in system for defending itself against these things. It is called the **immune system**.

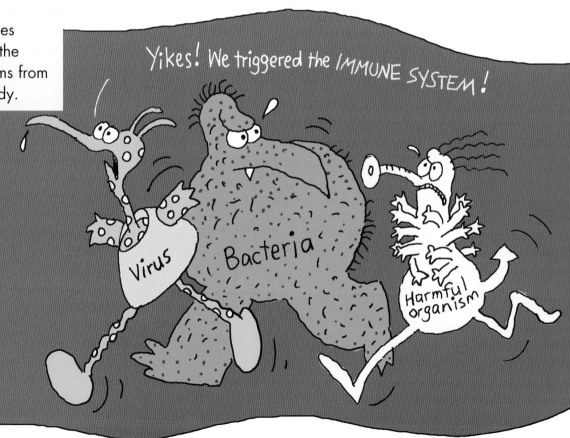

When harmful organisms enter the body, the immune system fights them off. Like most things, the immune system works best when we take good care of it. We can do this by having a healthy lifestyle and looking after our bodies so they continue to work well.

The more we learn about good health, the better! If we know what causes problems in our bodies, we can prevent disease, which is always better than having to cure it.

Find out more

Hand washing is the best way to keep from getting sick and spreading germs. How many times a day do you wash your hands? Find out how many germs could be on your hands ...

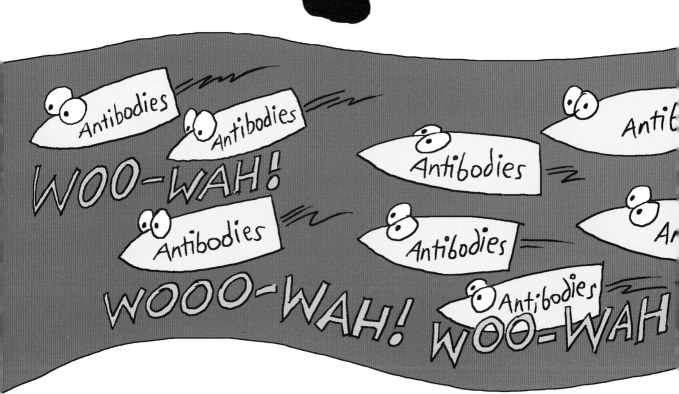

Ouch!
Getting those injections

A message from Dr Susan Gray

We need to have injections during the first four years of our life in order to build up our immune system. These injections are important because they protect us from some of the most serious diseases. The vaccine contains a dead or very weak dose of an organism that causes a disease – measles, for example. Our immune system immediately produces **antibodies** to fight the disease. These antibodies stay in our blood and protect us. If we are exposed to the disease, we will not get sick.

Vaccination is the best way to stop children from getting serious diseases and to stop diseases from spreading from one child to another. People older than your grandparents' generation were not so lucky. In those days, many children became very ill or even died from some serious diseases.

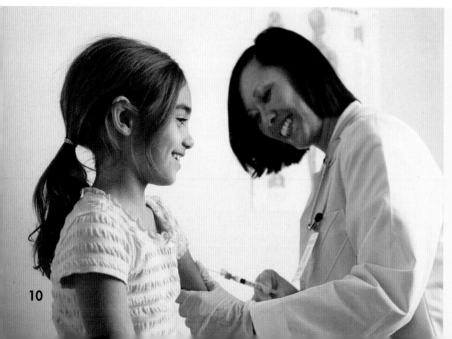

 Did you know?

Getting the measles can cause disabilities and even death, particularly among children. But in recent years, the number of children dying from measles in the world has fallen by 40 per cent as a result of immunisation programs.

Dangerous diseases		
Disease	**Which part of our body it affects**	**How we feel and look**
Tuberculosis (TB)	Lungs	Paleness; night sweats; loss of appetite, energy and weight; coughing up blood
Tetanus	Spinal cord	Extremely stiff jaw or neck; difficulty swallowing food and drink; painful fits
Poliomyelitis (Polio)	Central nervous system	Fever; sore throat; headache; vomiting; pain and stiffness; trembling legs and arms that may become paralysed
Diphtheria	Throat	Bleeding from nose; sores on the skin; severe cough; lumps on tonsils
Whooping cough	Throat	Severe cough that becomes worse at night; wheezing and difficulty breathing
Measles	Skin	Cough; runny eyes and nose; high temperature; skin rash
Chicken pox	Skin	Cough; runny eyes and nose; high temperature; skin rash with blisters

People were very afraid of getting cuts and scratches. They could get blood poisoning and die from these small wounds.

Because so many people died, scientists worked hard to develop vaccines that would prevent these diseases. The discovery of the **antibiotic** penicillin as a treatment for infections helped to keep people healthy. The chart above shows some of the most serious illnesses that can now be prevented by immunisation.

Think about ...

Think about a time when you were sick and needed medicine. What symptoms did you have? What kind of medicine did you take?

Fresh food

Fresh food is vital for good health, and the refrigerator is a very important invention when it comes to staying well. We can now keep food fresh until we want to eat it. Food can also be frozen so that it stays safe for a long time.

Many foods deteriorate or go bad quickly if they are not kept cold. Juice, milk, yogurt, cheeses and meats all need to be kept cool. That is why they are kept in the refrigerator. Eating food that has gone bad can make us very sick.

Very young children are more likely to get diseases from food that has gone bad because their immune system is still

developing. Bad food can make them ill or even kill them. Bottles that are used to feed babies need to be very clean and the milk has to be very fresh. Before there were refrigerators, many babies got very sick or died from drinking milk that had gone bad.

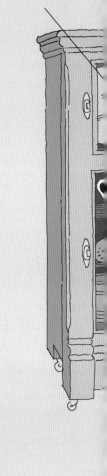

Block of ice kept in top compartment

Thinking like a scientist

Find out how long certain foods keep inside and outside the refrigerator.

You will need: Two glasses half-full with milk; an apple, chopped in half; two pieces of bread; 10 nuts; plastic wrap and bags.

What to do: Cover one glass of milk with plastic wrap; seal one-half of the apple, one slice of bread, and five nuts in plastic bags; and place in the refrigerator.

Ice chest from about 1900

Cold air is circulated into lower compartment

As the ice melts, a pipe carries the water to a tray underneath the ice chest.

The development of refrigeration

At first, people used ice chests to keep food cold. Ice chests were usually made of tin. Water was frozen to make blocks of ice, which were put into the ice chests. Milk and other food were kept near the ice. When the ice blocks melted, they were replaced with new ones.

Refrigerators were invented during the 1800s by many people in different countries working separately. The first refrigerators were big containers that kept food cool without using blocks of ice. They used kerosene or gas to make cold air to chill the food.

Electric refrigerators are even better. They were sold commercially from about 1911. People have been able to buy refrigerators to use in their homes since the start of the 1940s.

Leave the rest of the food out of the fridge in a place where it will not be interfered with. Again, cover the milk and seal the food in plastic bags. Tell your family not to touch any of the food.

Make signs to remind them of your experiment.

How long does each type of food last inside the refrigerator?

How long does each type of food last outside the refrigerator?

Which food lasted the longest outside the refrigerator?

Which food lasted the shortest time outside the refrigerator?

How can you tell?

Chapter 3

Allergic reactions

Some people react badly to certain foods, animals, plants or insect bites. This is called having an allergic reaction. Part of a healthy lifestyle is finding out about the things in our environment that might be harmful to us.

If you think you have an allergy, you should visit a doctor who will do tests to find out what you are allergic to. They can help you develop a plan to manage your allergy. This might include taking medicine or avoiding the things that cause the allergy. Some people never have an allergic reaction again because they stay away from the things that cause their allergy.

 Did you know?

Allergies can be inherited. If your parents have allergies, it is likely that you will have them too. The allergy you have may be different from the allergies of your parents.

Some of the things some people are allergic to

bee stings

shellfish

cats

eggs

peanuts

pollen

Living with allergies

Some people are allergic to certain foods and to **particles** carried by the wind. These people have allergic reactions when they eat the food or come into contact with the particles they are allergic to. An allergic reaction happens when your **immune system** overreacts and tries to fight ordinary things like pollen or wheat. Usually allergic reactions are quite mild, like sneezing or a runny nose, but sometimes they are life-threatening.

Juan: I have to be very careful if there are bees around. If a bee stings me, my throat swells up and I find it hard to breathe. I have to get to a doctor right away to get an injection to make the lump go down.

Jamal: Every spring I get hayfever. My nose runs and I sneeze a lot, my eyes get red and itchy, and I'm tired and have headaches. Pollen causes my hayfever, so Mum finds out the pollen count every day in spring on the Internet. If it's too high, I try to stay indoors. I also stay inside on windy days. I use a nasal spray to help lessen the symptoms, and sometimes I take pills.

Some of the common allergens are:

- dust mites, or the tiny insects that live in dust
- dry skin flakes, saliva, urine or other things from some animals
- grass, flower and tree pollen
- mould and mildew
- foods, including milk, wheat, soy, eggs, seafood, nuts and **legumes**.

Did you know?

An EpiPen is an injector that can be used to give medicine by people who are not trained as doctors or nurses. This is because the medicine needs to be given as quickly as possible once an allergic reaction begins. Otherwise, the person could die.

Carmen: I'm allergic to wheat. If I eat a slice of bread or a biscuit or any other food containing wheat, I get hives, which are itchy red spots on my skin. The doctor said that children with a wheat allergy often outgrow it, so I'm hoping this will be the case for me.

Ella: I am allergic to peanuts. If I eat the tiniest bit of peanut, my tongue swells up and I start to choke. I feel really ill. Dad has to look at all the food labels to check if there are any peanuts or peanut oil in the food. Everywhere I go, an adult needs to have a special injector called an EpiPen. This has medicine in it that will stop my allergic reaction.

Did you know?

Asthma ranks among the ten most common reasons for seeing a doctor. Up to one in four children, one in seven teenagers, and one in ten adults will have an asthma attack at some time in their lives.

Living with asthma

Some people regularly get asthma. Asthma is a disease that affects people's lungs and makes it hard for them to breathe. Sometimes asthma attacks are so severe that people need to go to the hospital. Asthma can be life-threatening.

Asthma is caused mainly by allergies to mould, chemicals, pollen, tobacco smoke and the dust mites that live in carpets, bedding and furniture. It is common and also tends to run in families.

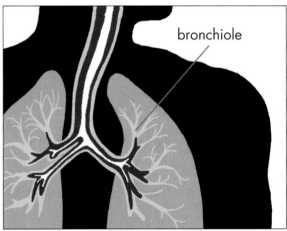

bronchiole

During an asthma attack, the bronchioles swell, making it hard for the person to get enough air.

Did you know?
Inhalers are handheld portable devices that can be used by people with asthma to deliver medication directly to their lungs. Inhalers can provide quick relief, or they can help to control the symptoms of asthma over a longer period.

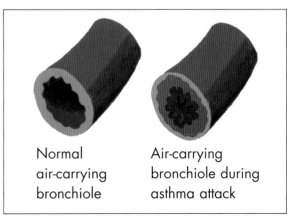

Normal air-carrying bronchiole

Air-carrying bronchiole during asthma attack

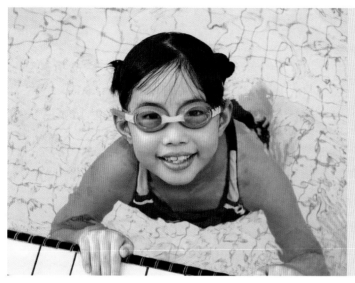

Tien: I have asthma. I have a bad cough all the time, but it gets worse in the middle of the night. I feel as if I can't breathe properly and my chest hurts. Mum or Dad has to sit me up in bed and stay with me. Once I had to go to the hospital. Dad takes me to swimming lessons now. Swimming will make my lungs stronger so I will be able to breathe better.

Hector: My asthma is worse in spring when the wind blows seeds and pollen around in the air. When I start to feel an asthma attack coming on, I have to use an inhaler. I inhale two puffs, which helps me to breathe more easily. I am training for the basketball team.

Lina: I have asthma. I have to take asthma medication every day, and I have to be careful about exercising. If I get winded, it's hard for me to catch my breath and I might start to wheeze. This means I make a high-pitched raspy sound when I try to breathe. I am short of breath, but if I rest for a while, I can keep exercising.

Chapter 4

Living a full life

Advances in science and medicine have played a large part in improving the health of many people. In the same way, researchers have come up with ways of helping people with disabilities to see, hear, walk or communicate. In some cases equipment and machines are used to help people.

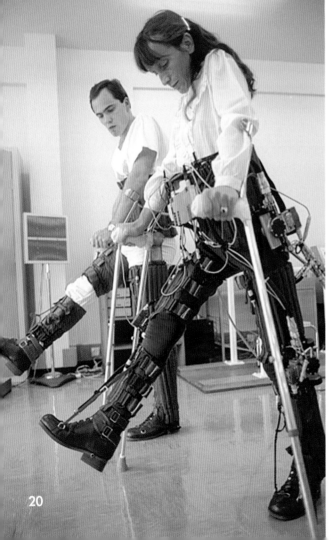

Find out more

A prosthesis is an artificial replacement for a body part such as an arm or a leg.

The science of robotics is making amazing advances in how artificial body parts work. Find out about the benefits for people who have a prosthesis.

The bionic ear

Last night, Lola took part in her school play. She was able to speak her lines and hear what the other actors were saying. She was also able to hear the audience clapping. At one stage in her life, none of this would have been possible for Lola because she was born with a hearing **impairment**.

Lola and many other hearing-impaired children can thank a team of scientists for opening up the world of sound to them. This miracle resulted from the invention of the cochlear implant, which is known as the bionic ear.

The bionic ear comes in several parts. One part, which is smaller than a fingernail, is put into the inner ear. The other parts are worn outside the ear. A coil that carries sound is held in position against the skin by a magnet, and a microphone is worn behind the ear. The speech processor can be carried in a pocket, belt pouch or harness.

Dr Graeme Clark led a team of scientists in Australia that invented the bionic ear. The idea for the device came from experiments with a piece of grass and a seashell. The first implant was done in 1978.

Dr Clark's research took 37 years and involved 175 scientists. The bionic ear has restored hearing to hundreds of thousands of children and adults around the world.

Since then, scientists in the United States have developed a bionic ear that can pick up radio waves that people cannot normally hear. These radio waves are changed into sound for adults or children with a severe hearing impairment.

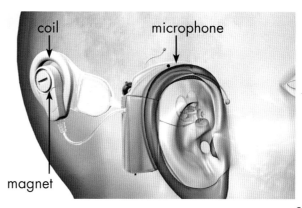

coil microphone

magnet

Aiming to be the best

A surfing champion: Bethany Hamilton

Bethany Hamilton is a champion surfer who lives on the island of Kauai in Hawaii. In 2003 she was surfing off a beach when she was attacked by a 14-foot tiger shark. This attack left Bethany, at age 13, with one arm severed. However, she was determined to enter the water again and follow her dream of becoming an even better surfer. Since her accident, Bethany has competed in many surfing finals.

▼ Gold medallist Ellie Cole of Australia poses on the podium at the medal ceremony for Women's 100m Backstroke at the 2016 Paralympic Games in Rio de Janeiro, Brazil.

A Paralympic champion: Ellie Cole

When she was a child, Ellie Cole took swimming lessons after her right leg was amputated. Swimming was a sport she could do where no one tried to stop her because she only had one leg. She was soon competing in international championships. At the 2012 Paralympics, Ellie won four gold and two bronze medals, and at the Rio Paralympics in 2016 she won five more medals – two gold, three silver and a bronze. The Paralympic Games is the world's top sporting competition for athletes with a disability. The games are held in the same year as the Olympic Games, with the word "para" meaning parallel to, or alongside, the Olympic Games.

Glossary

allergen anything that might cause someone to have an allergic reaction

antibiotic a drug that kills

antibodies antibodies are found in the blood. Their job is to find germs that should not be inside your body and mark them by sticking to them. Your body then knows the germs are there and can begin to fight them.

bacteria tiny organisms that are present everywhere; some bacteria cause diseases in humans, but many others are very useful to us

immune system the human body's built-in system for defending itself against harmful viruses, bacteria and organisms

impairment a disability associated with one of the body's features or senses

legume plants such as peas, beans and lentils

particles tiny specks such as dust or pollen

vaccination a type of modified virus or bacteria put into a body's immune system to prevent the onset of a disease

virus a tiny infectious agent that can replicate itself only within a living host cell

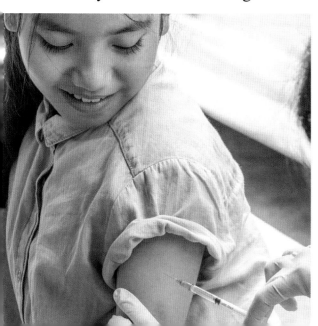

Index